Private Lives of Public Figures

Written by the editors of* SPY *and Drew Friedman

St. Martin's Press ▼ New York

To my wonderful wife, Kathy.

Special thanks to Kurt Andersen, Joanne Gruber, E. Graydon Carter, Nicki Gostin, Alexander Isley, B. W. Honeycutt, Christiaan Kuypers, & Jim Fitzgerald.

Additional material by Drew Friedman & K. Bidus.

Also by Drew Friedman (Coauthored by Josh Alan Friedman):
Any Similarity to Persons Living or Dead Is Purely Coincidental
Warts and All

All of the cartoons in this book previously appeared in *Spy* magazine except for those appearing on pages 19, 34, 39, 47, 49, 51, 52, 62, 74, and 78.

Design by Jaye Zimet

Library of Congress Cataloging-in-Publication Data

Friedman, Drew.
Private lives of public figures / Drew Friedman.
p. cm.
From the pages of Spy magazine published in New York.
ISBN 0-312-09366-7
1. Celebrities—Caricatures and cartoons. 2. American wit and humor, Pictorial. 3. Spy (New York, N.Y.) I. Spy (New York, N.Y.) II. Title.
NC1429.F6694A4 1993
741.5'973—dc20 93-3521
CIP

First edition: July 1993

10 9 8 7 6 5 4 3 2 1

Introduction

Before you read this introduction for *Private Lives of Public Figures,* let me just inform you that I'm Gilbert Gottfried. I'd hate for you to read it and find out at the end who wrote it. I mean, I'd hate for you to read it and then say, "Damn, I just read an introduction by Gilbert Gottfried. I never read his stuff. I have no respect for his opinion." Anyway, you've been warned.

You know when you have a very high fever, about 106°? You feel nauseated and queasy, then, out of weakness, fall asleep. You start having very disturbing dreams, then you wake up drenched in sweat, run to the toilet, and puke. Well, looking at Drew Friedman's cartoons, especially those that appear in *Spy,* reminds me of one of those dreams. I don't always puke after looking at one of his cartoons. Sometimes I feel like I need a shower immediately, but that's me. You might be one of those people who laughs at this stuff. If so, read this book.

—Gilbert Gottfried

(But I guess I already told you that.)

Private Drives

On a search for new musical inspiration, David Byrne unexpectedly runs into Paul Simon.

Presidential candidate Pat Buchanan readies himself to plunge into the campaign-trail melting pot.

Dick Clark gives his *American Bandstand* replacement a few pointers.

Assistant District Attorney John F. Kennedy, Jr., prepares to retake the bar exam.

Brandon Tartikoff brainstorms in his new office at Paramount Pictures.

Developer Mortimer Zuckerman decides to scale back his proposed Columbus Circle project.

Geraldo Rivera diligently researches material for a future episode of his television show.

The Reverend Al Sharpton planning new investigative strategies.

At the Middle East peace conference, Secretary of State Baker discusses the history of the Jewish state.

Father Bruce Ritter avails himself of some vocational training before embarking on a new career.

Former funnyman Dan Aykroyd chooses movie scripts for future roles.

Senator Alfonse D'Amato confers with a cochairman of his campaign steering committee.

White House Chief of Staff John Sununu discusses policy matters with colleagues at a Cabinet meeting.

Joyce Carol Oates deep in research for her next book.

Dan Quayle and advisers plot last-minute campaign strategy.

Director John Hughes holds a preproduction meeting for his next blockbuster.

President Reagan raises a new issue with General Secretary Gorbachev.

Private Pastimes

George Bush shares his humor with an appreciative golfing buddy.

Former Met Rusty Staub gives Keith Hernandez a taste of something delicious.

Lee Atwater entertains some friends with a Negro spiritual.

Sofia Coppola spends Oscar night with family, friends, and fans.

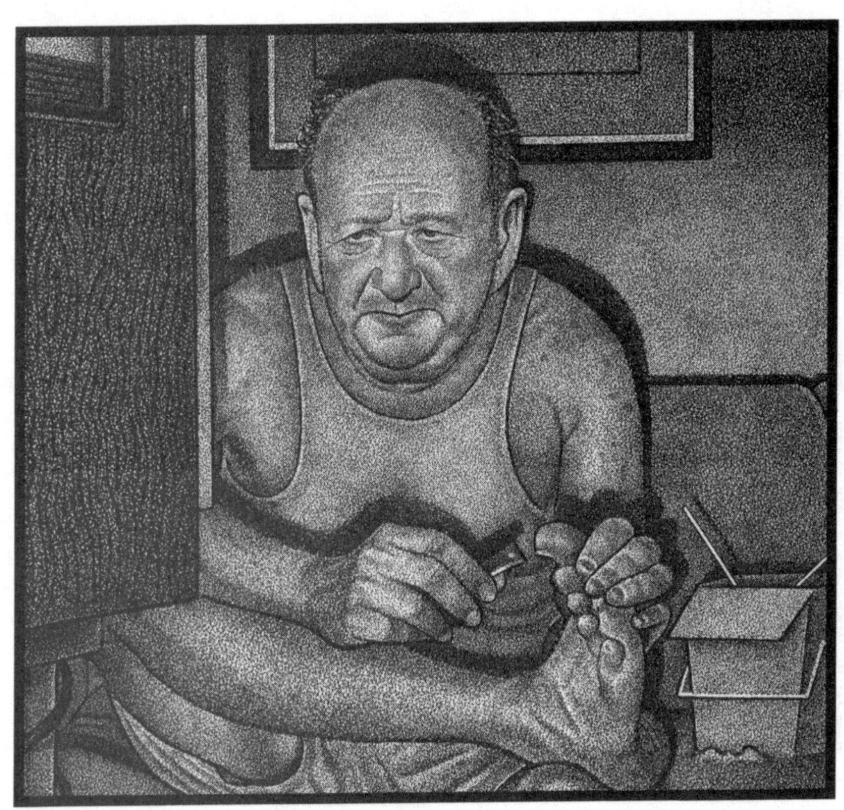

Ed Koch at his home in the heart of the greatest, most glamorous city on Earth.

Supreme Court plaintiff Jerry Falwell, in high spirits, pays his mother a surprise visit.

After a rough day on the campaign trail, Gary Hart relaxes with his top aides.

Former headmistress Jean Harris enjoys a taste of freedom.

City Council President Andy Stein begins his day with some fastidious grooming.

Supreme Court justice David Souter does some late-night reading at home.

Guns 'N' Roses' Slash goes home for the holidays.

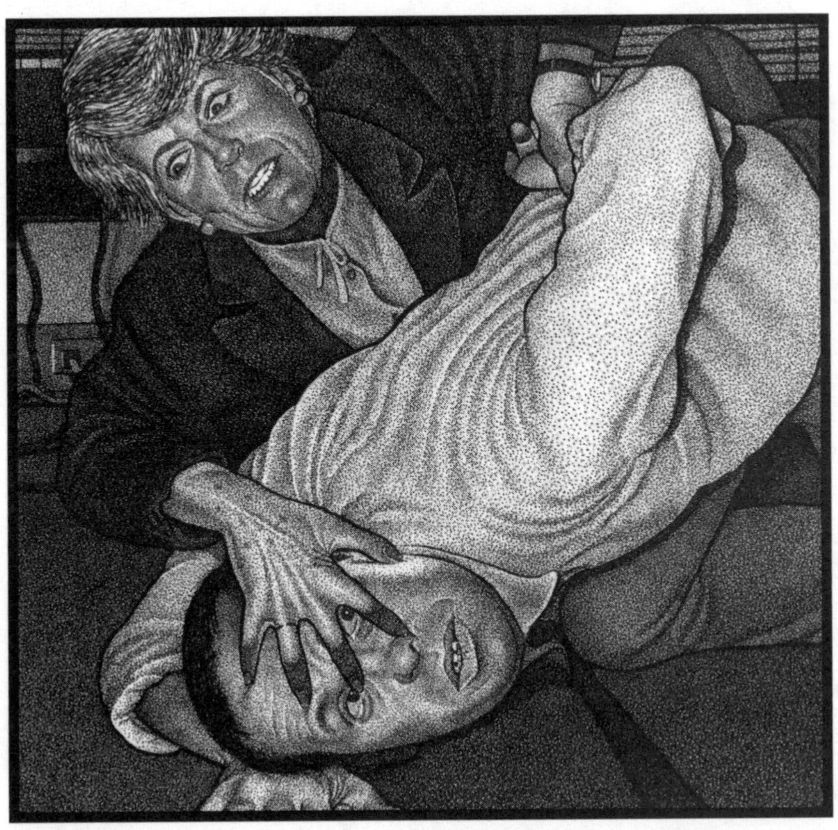

Geraldine Ferraro shares a quiet moment with husband John Zaccaro.

America's second family enjoys some Sunday-afternoon quality time at home.

Vice President Gore entertains at an end-of-school-year party for Chelsea Clinton and her friends.

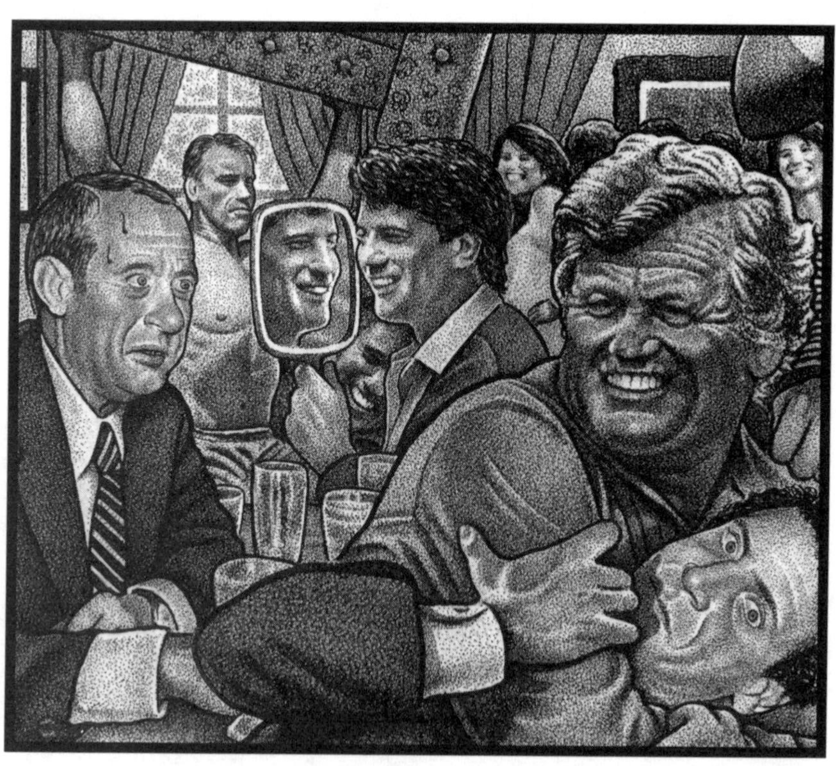

Mario Cuomo has his in-laws over for dinner.

Howard Stern boogaloos Saturday nights at the local B'nai B'rith.

Hillary Clinton demonstrates her commitment to traditional family values.

Private Disorders

Michael Jackson chats with some friends from out of town.

Senator and Mrs. Edward Kennedy head home from a New Year's Eve party in Georgetown.

Oliver Stone rehearses his Oscar acceptance speech.

Longtime Yankee manager Billy Martin prepares for the start of another season.

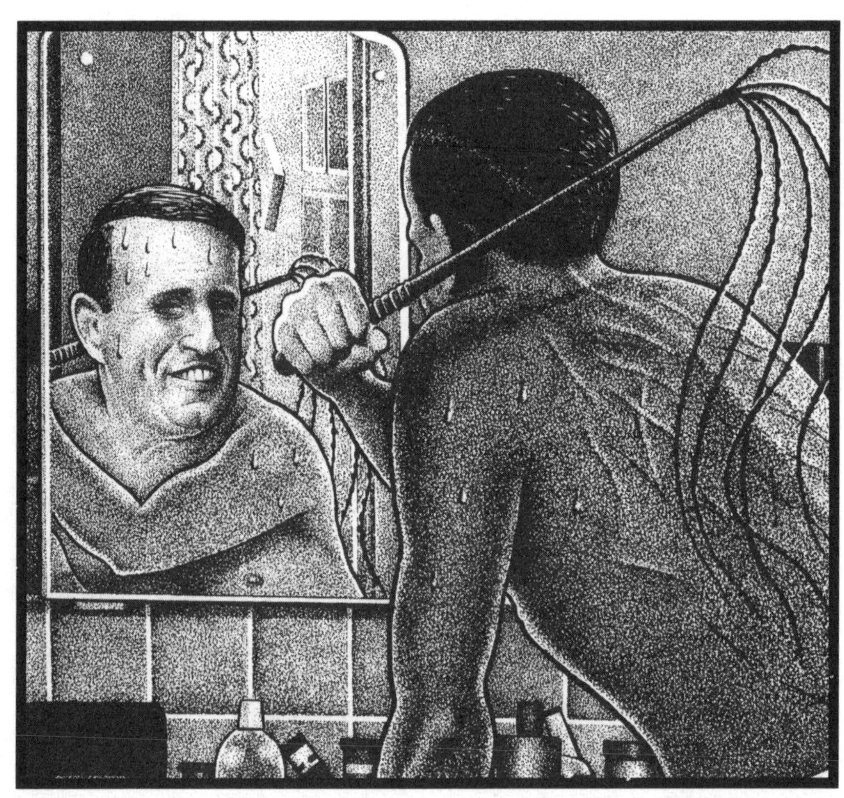

Prosecutor-turned-politician Rudolph Giuliani enjoys his morning workout.

Michael Jackson confers with trusted advisers on the chances that an asteroid may collide with Earth in the next century.

Jim Bakker rehearses with his lawyers for his next court appearance.

First Lady of Radio Barbara Bush enchants children with the tale of Red Riding Hood, complete with portrayal of the Big Bad Wolf.

H. Ross Perot's presidential nominating convention, back home in Dallas.

Bubbles the Chimp seeks professional help in adjusting to his increasingly bizarre home life.

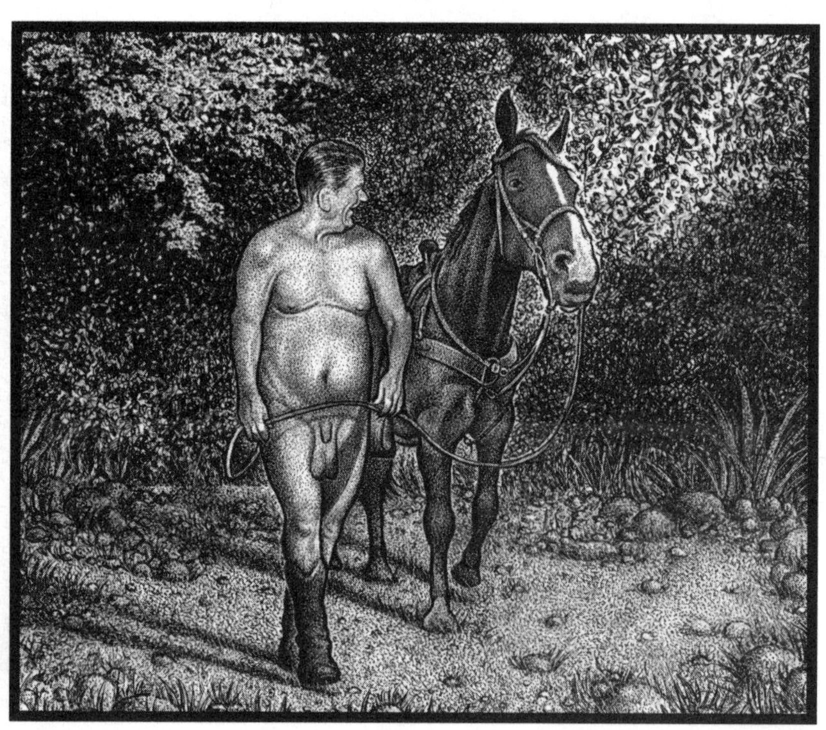

Unbeknownst to a slumbering Nancy, Ronald Reagan takes an early morning constitutional.

Private Crimes

Successful, important entertainer-educator-author Bill Cosby is never too busy to consider a financial opportunity.

Leona Helmsley assists husband Harry with a letter to the federal prosecutor.

U.S. Attorney General Ed Meese discusses his professional future with his boss.

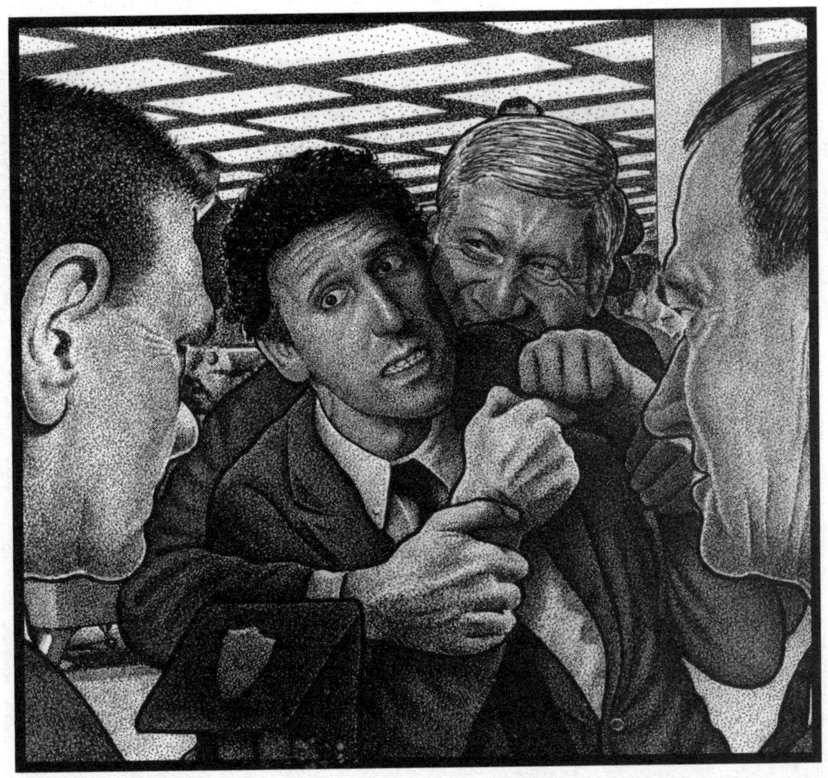

Drexel Burnham CEO Fred Joseph encourages his Beverly Hills colleague Mike Milken to use his own best judgment regarding the federal investigation.

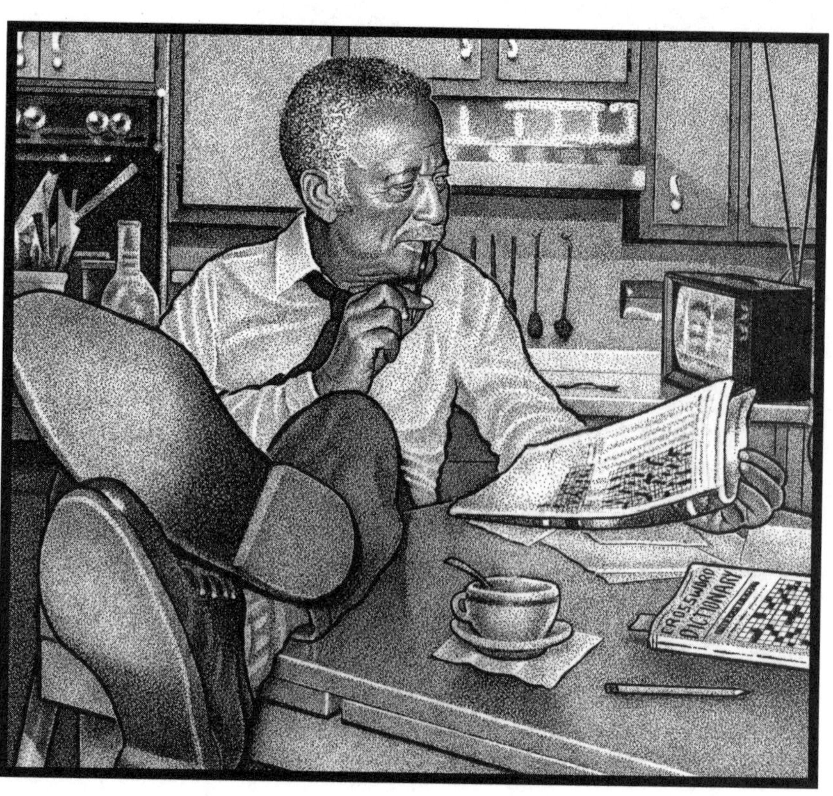

New York mayor David Dinkins prepares his 1989 tax return.

Donald Jr., Ivanka, and little Eric call their dad to wish him a happy Father's Day.

First Lady Nancy Reagan begins preparations for leaving the White House.

Publisher S. I. Newhouse makes some top-level management decisions.

Natalie Cole records her most "Unforgettable" single.

Private Slimes

Warren Beatty and Jack Nicholson spend some quality time with their children at a Lakers game.

Penthouse publisher Bob Guccione fills up his water bed the ultraclassy way.

William Kennedy Smith and Mike Tyson discuss their plans for the evening.

Candidate Donald Trump discusses important national issues with close advisers.

John Cardinal O'Connor makes a totally impromptu visit to the Bronx, thrilling stunned passersby.

Justice Clarence Thomas greets the day before heading off to work.

After a hard day of campaigning, Bill Clinton teaches Karenna Gore how to play the saxophone.

Private Dotage

Johnny Carson and his wife enjoy retirement.

The First Lady has a special surprise for this year's trick-or-treaters.

Dean Martin and Jerry Lewis discuss plans for a professional comeback.

Supreme Court justices William H. Rehnquist and Sandra Day O'Connor share a warm, friendly moment with colleague Thurgood Marshall.

Richard Nixon and George Steinbrenner welcome Elliot Abrams and Cap Weinberger to their secret fraternity.

Ed Koch, Harry Helmsley, and Rudolph Bing enjoy their dinners amid the Yuletide festivities at The "21" Club.

The Rolling Stones celebrate thirty years of Rock & Roll.

Ronald Reagan celebrates his 80th birthday.

Drew Friedman has been contributing "Private Lives of Public Figures" to *Spy* magazine since its inception. His comics and illustrations also appear in *Raw, Details, The New York Times, Rolling Stone, Premiere, National Lampoon, Mother Jones, Spin,* and *Entertainment Weekly,* among other publications. His work has been collected into two anthologies, *Any Similarity to Persons Living or Dead Is Purely Coincidental* and *Warts and All,* and is featured on MTV's *Liquid Television* and in the *News of the Weird* books. He currently resides in the mountains of Pennsylvania with his wife and collaborator, Kathy, and their five little ones (four cats and a dog).